To Kelly!
Embrace u
chaos! *

THRIVING
IN CHAOS

Lessons Learned as a Corporate Marketer

Joanne Gore

THRIVING IN CHAOS

Lessons Learned as a Corporate Marketer

Joanne Gore

quratebooks.com

Book Creation Service

It's time you tell your story

https://rsprintingsolutions.com/book-creation-services/

THRIVING IN CHAOS
Lessons Learned as a Corporate Marketer
Joanne Gore

Published by Qurate Books Pvt. Ltd.

© Joanne Gore

First Published in 2023

ISBN: 978-93-58980-43-1

Qurate Books Pvt. Ltd.
Goa 403523, India
www.quratebooks.com
Tel: 1800-210-6527, Email: info@quratebooks.com

Foreword

As long as I have known Joanne Gore, she has been a source of enthusiasm, joy, hope, and evangelism. Whether we are talking about empowering people new to the communication industries or working on projects together, Joanne is always about the active, positive way forward, even as the usual array of challenges comes to the surface. The story of how she evolved into the energetic problem-solver I know is filled with challenges and learnings.

If you search book catalogues, you find a million stories of how people find their profession. Some are born into it. Some discover a passion early on and build their life plan to pursue it. Some are thrust into situations that force quick learning, building experience, character, and empathy along their business journey. This is Joanne's story.

In this book, Joanne shares the highs and lows that guided her development from a young woman with high moral values and a desire to grow to a successful businesswoman. She shares the harsh realities of growing up in an era when bullying was sometimes encouraged as character-building and how that shaped her. Then, diving into adulthood, she shares the yo-yo experience that women in business often face.

Multiple trips through hurdles leading to continuing successes, Joanne lets you walk in her shoes. You see the challenges and how she found a plan. You follow her as she creates the best path, leveraging her hard-won experience. She shares her learnings, so readers have a quick reference guide to options when they face the same challenges.

If you are at the beginning of your path into business, no matter what industry segment appeals to you, this book sets you up to be prepared for the things life throws at all of us. If you are already on your journey and have faced bullying, discrimination, or had your motives questioned as you pursue your goals, this book brings information on overcoming and provides a shining light to guide you through the dark times.

There is an amazing world waiting for you! Joanne dares you to dream but also to execute. I hope you take her advice.

Pat McGrew
Managing Director
McGrew Group, Inc.

Preface

Appearances misguide.

My profession demands a balancing act between aggressiveness, assertiveness, and being a "yes person" to please everyone. Ultimately, my clients bestow their faith in me for the person I am, the knowledge I bring, and the work I deliver.

I'm Joanne, and I believe in myself.

I've delivered against all odds, gotten to the core of the challenges and problems I faced, and emerged victorious — most of the time.

I roll up my sleeves and don't rest until the work is done to my satisfaction. Owning my s*** and surpassing expectations is a trait both my colleagues and my clients expect – and value.

How did I go from being an "artsy" designer to that fierce female in male-dominated industries? Did all the testosterone rub off on me? How could it not? As the *go-to person*, I became a taskmaster, a badass, and a proud alpha female.

Along the way, I opened myself up to being misjudged and misunderstood. What could I do about it? Nothing. I am here to look at the bigger picture, the larger canvas, and to solve the marketing challenges plaguing software, hardware, manufacturing, and print companies.

"What you do has a far greater impact than what you say," said Stephen Covey. I'd say that sums it up.

When I am introspective, I often question how I became who I am today. A tumultuous childhood left me burdened with responsibilities at a young age. I grew up quickly, withstood bullies and saboteurs, and battled stereotypes.

I became determined to move ahead and stand up, never giving into the situation, challenges, or discriminations I faced.

I often reflect on my brother's Bar Mitzvah portrait (circa 1966), painted by an artist who didn't have hands, who instead had learned to paint with his feet. This portrait is a constant reminder of how any obstacle can be overcome with the right mindset. Imagine the determination and passion it must have taken, especially in that era, to produce such a life-like work of art. It was almost haunting. Has this portrait played an important part in shaping me?

How could it not?

I evolved through the eighties and nineties to the crossing of the millennium. I lived through the technological boom – from the dawn of the internet to the subsequent dot-com bust, the 2020 global pandemic – and everything in between. I welcomed every new challenge thrown at me.

I embrace these changes to learn, further evolve, and fill a never-ending fuel tank for myself.

No matter which business you are in, you need to maintain solid relationships with your employees, customers, vendors, and associates, and I'm no exception.

Over time, I realised that as you get closer to the people in your business sphere, they spot the character you are made of.

Eventually, it hit me like a lightning bolt!

It's not about what I do.

It's about how I help.

What resonates with me is hard-work, resourcefulness, sincerity, integrity, and a *can-do* attitude – seasoned with creativity, empathy, and brutal honesty. All these reflect in my work.

I cannot tell you how many umpteen times I heard, "You need to write a book, Joanne! Your story is just too incredible!"

While flattered, I never felt ready. I never felt worthy.

This book is a result of the confidence and faith shown in me by my clients, my family, and my colleagues as I ventured on a journey to help others.

What is crucial to understand is how I balanced a mind always teetering between creativity and analytics to find that sweet spot in my work.

Linear, pragmatic thinking helps me derive intelligence from data and arrive at the right decisions in the numbers game. As W. Edwards Deming said, "In God we trust. All others must bring data." This approach results in practical workflows and processes across all aspects of my life, both personal and business, helping me squeeze every drop out of every minute.

My creative brain bursts with colourful spontaneity and non-linear thinking; tapping into it unleashes my mind to visualise scenarios and connect dots that many cannot see. This combination has helped me arrive at work hacks (aka strategies) that you can adapt as you travel your own career path.

I hope to inspire you to thrive with strategies that free you to pursue your passions and stay true to yourself while navigating the chaotic aspects of business – and life.

It doesn't matter if you are from a small town, economically or socially strong, or have a degree. All you need is the ability to welcome challenges, seek solutions, and not get bogged down in getting it all done.

There's nothing like climbing the ranks in a male-dominated world. People my age will tell you, "It's so much better for women today." And it's true. But we still have far to go. Today's intolerance for yesterday's bad behaviour did not exist, and the only things to get cancelled were television shows.

Good or bad, those experiences helped shape me into the fierce female I am today.

With this book, I hope to inspire a new generation to seek out what makes them happy and find value in every experience.

Students of all ages will find ideas and perspectives that go beyond academics. Ultimately, they'll get a better understanding of how the business world operates and how to adapt to its practical aspects while pursuing their passions.

People in mid-career should find this book motivating them to explore the paths they have always considered but were hesitant to pursue.

Professionals sitting on a massive pile of experience cultivated over many years may be inspired to pursue side-hustles to feed their entrepreneurial appetite.

Dare to dream; dare to go for it.

Finally, as Marshall Goldsmith writes in his book, "What got you here won't get you there," it's time we up our game.

I have done it consistently throughout my life.

Now it's your turn.

About the Author

"Twenty years from now, you will be more disappointed by the things you didn't do than by the ones you did do. So, throw off the bowlines. Sail away from the safe harbour. Catch the trade winds in your sails. Explore. Dream. Discover."

-Mark Twain

Born in Montreal, Canada, in the mid-sixties, I grew up with both French and English as the country's official languages; this bi-lingual advantage has stayed with me to this day.

Montreal was referred to as "Canada's *Cultural Capital*" by Monocle Magazine. The city is Canada's centre for French-language television productions, radio, theatre, film, multimedia, and print publishing. The *Quartier Latin* is a neighbourhood crowded with cafés animated by this literary and musical activity. Montreal's many cultural communities have given it a distinct local culture.

School was different back in the '70s. Students focused on the basics: reading, writing, mathematics, and, of course, French. We also learned how to write longhand and took great pride in our *penmanship* (at least I did). Back in the '70s, the personal computer was still very much in the realm of science fiction; students learned in the classroom, in the library – and at home. We did our homework with pen, pencil, and notebooks; and got our information from encyclopaedias, books, journals, magazines, brochures – basically anything printed.

As a child, I grew up with a curious mind; always looking for the edge, always one step ahead, and always soaking up what was around. My formal education had a somewhat informal start when my parents took me on a trip to Jamaica at the young age of 6. Unlike today's family vacation options that include kids' clubs, camps, and scheduled activities - parents had to find ways to entertain their children. In my case, my parents had become friendly with the hotel staff. They were especially close with the manager of the hotel, thanks to their repeated trips in the past.

* *

As a child, I grew up with a curious mind; always looking for the edge, always one step ahead, and always soaking up what was around.

* *

School in Jamaica

We were there for a few weeks. We visited all the tourist spots, played in the pool, and participated in any and all on-site activities. But let's face it. Parents deserve some R&R too. So, for a few hours a day, they sent me to school. I was in heaven.

With my parents in Jamaica

With my mother and brother in Jamaica

Though I was in kindergarten back home in Montreal, I was thrilled to be going to Grade One in Jamaica. A child's mind is like a sponge, they say. It can absorb and grasp faster than what one does as you age. In two weeks, I'd learned to read and was consuming books at a grade 2 level.

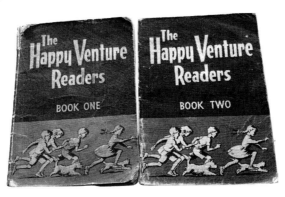

The following year, as I was getting ready to officially start Grade one at Logan School in Montreal, I was instead put into a split Grade one/two class. The year after that, I was placed straight into Grade Three, igniting an achievement fire that fuels me to this day.

By the time I entered Grade Seven, my final year of elementary school, the province had introduced French immersion as an option beginning in Grade One. To fast-track into the high-school bilingual program (and receive our bilingual certificates), most of us spent our last year of elementary school completely immersed in French. Every subject, with the exception of English, was taught in French, including math, geography, history, and even Phys-ed. If you were caught speaking English in the schoolyard, cafeteria, or hallways, you risked detention.

Math was a subject I was good at in French immersion, and when it was time to enter high school as a Grade Eight student, I was placed in an advanced Math course. This worked well for me again. I continued to leap-frog my way through high school; by the time I started my eleventh and graduating year, I already had multiple college courses completed and a French advantage.

It was time for me to choose where to attend CEGEP (aka: College). It was time for me to decide what I wanted to do with the rest of my life.

I was sixteen.

There was always a conflict in my mind between art and computer science. While I had won a poster contest in Grade Two, I'm not an illustrator. I honestly can't draw my way out of a paper bag. However, I can look at something and envision the layout for how the image, text, and negative space should be structured in the most optimum and creative manner. I call it *logical creativity*.

This creative/analytical divide in my brain was made apparent in all sorts of personality and IQ tests throughout my life – with a 50:50 split right down the middle as a common result. Embracing this dichotomy of capabilities, I finally chose Graphic Design as my major.

I graduated 3 years later with a love of typography, a diploma in Graphic Design Technology, and a job offer to work as a graphic designer for a printing company 500km away in Toronto, Ontario.

I was nineteen years old.

During the early years of my career, I cut my teeth in dark rooms, on stat machines, changing font disks, and running art departments. In a pinch, I even ran an AB Dick printing press.

Understanding the creative mindset helps me communicate with today's designers on a different level because I speak their language. Combining that capability with corporate marketing acumen and an ability to strategize and connect the dots, I discovered how to help companies take off. This fusion of marketing, technology, and creativity would come to span nearly every B2B (Business-to-Business) vertical industry, from scrappy startups to established enterprises.

* *

There was always a conflict in my mind between — art and computers. While I embraced creativity, I visualized numbers and patterns.

* *

Writing this book not only inspired me to reflect on how I became the person I am today, but also to channel (and share) those reflections into lessons learned.

My parents separated when I was just eight, shortly after my Romanian-born maternal grandmother moved into our Montreal duplex with me and my mother, who returned to work as a legal secretary. They divorced when I was ten, and my father moved to Toronto. Before marrying each other, my parents had already been married and divorced. This was the second marriage for them both.

Technically, I'm an only child surrounded by a very complex family structure, including three half-siblings – two sisters from my father's first marriage - and a half-brother from my mother's first marriage.

Shortly after I turned 16, my father, who had relocated to Toronto 6 years earlier, remarried. Just two short months later, he died from a massive heart attack.

About to graduate high school, financial responsibilities were ever-looming. Thankfully, the 3-year intensive CEGEP program I was accepted into was (and remains) government funded. While that means no tuition fees, I was on the hook for supplies and equipment – from specialty instruments like rapidographs, to set-squares, cameras, darkroom equipment, and, most importantly, a professional drafting table. I didn't know it at the time, but I was just getting ready for much bigger battles ahead.

I can't remember a time when I wasn't finding ways to make some extra cash. I gave manicures to my mom's friends, worked at Harvey's (Canada's version of McDonald's), and worked in retail sales (which I despised). On the way to a full-fledged job in my chosen profession, I switched and swapped many times. I've worked triple-shifts and book-ended full-time jobs with morning and evening freelance gigs and side-hustles. Sleep was a luxury, and I often thought, why waste time when I could put it to work for me?

For a girl like me, who survived a major car accident when I was just six months old that left everyone wondering if I'd ever walk or talk, these life experiences were the beginning of a journey that would lead me to become the fierce (sometimes feared) female I am today.

I've overcome being blindsided a few times in my life. One particular setback was when I realized my husband had wiped out all our finances, racked up tens of thousands of dollars in debt, and defrauded our bank. The money set aside for our three boys to attend University was gone. Credit cards (in my name) were maxed out, and so was the mortgage fund (yup, I was on the hook for that too).

I was responsible for re-paying hundreds of thousands of dollars and restoring a crippled credit score.

My husband was placed under house arrest, and our marriage ended. It broke our family. It broke me until I pushed through and regained control of my family, my finances, and my life.

I eventually met another man who added two more boys to the mix. Together, we became a family of seven, including five boys between the ages of 8 and 14. He helped us get through some very dark times and became a father-figure to my boys when they needed it most. It gives us great pride and immense satisfaction that all five of our children are University graduates, embarking on careers in finance, marketing, entertainment, business – and even graphic design.

Career-wise, as mentioned earlier, Harvey's was the job that supported me through college. My career, however, started in a print shop, then wound its way into software and tech. When I ultimately launched my business, I embraced all my roles as a corporate marketer, especially my years at one of Canada's most successful software companies of its time – Delrina, makers of WinFaxPRO.

Delrina was my first corporate marketing role. I was hired for my design, print, and production expertise. As such, I was responsible for meeting deadlines and establishing global print standards. I travelled to the UK, Ireland, and across the US and Canada to attend press approvals and institute guidelines.

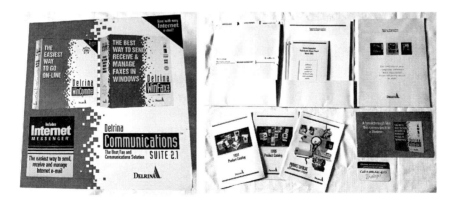

During press checks, my French came in handy since our printer was located in Montreal. While I could communicate with the press operators in French, proving myself as someone who knew their way around a printing press was an obstacle I needed to overcome quickly.

I didn't need the loupe (magnifying glass), as my young naked eye could spot hickeys and any colour out of registration easily. Using this *super-power*, I quickly earned the press operator's respect – once he got over his initial scepticism and dis-belief.

Throughout a corporate career that spanned three decades, I worked as a marketing coordinator, print production manager and specialist, and ultimately global marketing director. I got bounced around the tech industry quite a lot, falling victim to the dot-com bust and a constant flux of mergers and acquisitions.

I've worked, travelled, and managed trade shows and events where I was the only female amidst a team of men. I had to learn to speak their language to deliver my results effectively. This fostered my resilience and set me on a course that would forever change who I helped, how I helped, and why it mattered.

I developed a very thick skin - and very colourful language.

The fighter in me was my inspiration — the hunger to learn and excel opened new doors. As someone who always had to prove my worth, the times ahead looked exciting.

Joining Avanti, a Print MIS (management information system) software company in 2014 became another turning point. After years at an arms-length from the print industry, I returned to my roots. Finally, I found my nirvana – Software, Print, B2B – and the flexibility to continue working from home 2 – 3 days a week.

All this continued until their acquisition by Ricoh (here we go again!) and the subsequent launch of my new business. In the year 2017, Joanne Gore Communications – a full-service and virtually-run B2B agency was formed; in 2019, we incorporated. Three months later, the world went into lockdown – and the company went global.

Joanne Gore Communications (JGC) helps software, hardware, manufacturing, and print companies stretch their marketing dollars, pinpoint their quickest time to money, and attract a new generation of business – with programs that generate awareness, engagement, and growth. In the following pages, you will learn how I embraced the lessons learned as a corporate marketer to thrive in the chaos of business – and life.

Buckle up!

Joanne Gore

* *

*"Life is ten percent what happens to you
and ninety percent how you respond to it."*

Lou Holtz

Contents

Change… it's all around us

"Change is inevitable. Growth is optional."

- John Maxwell

Universally, if the core objective of any business is to make a profit, then the process to achieve that must be razor-sharp. Unfortunately, solving one problem or pain-point that's impacting profitability often exposes others you didn't even know existed. And while everyone is engrossed in solving these issues, they often fail to pivot as their business and client-base evolve.

That's where JGC comes in.

At Joanne Gore Communications, we help you figure out *who* you help, *how* you help, and why it *matters* – today.

In this hyper-chaotic world, having a great infrastructure is not enough. Having the best ERP (Enterprise Resource Planning), CRM (Customer Relationship Management), or manufacturing practices will not get you your dream customers. But having the right lead generation strategy aligned to your ideal customer will hasten up the process to reach your desired goals.

When you know how to review and change the goalposts based on what's trending, where the wind is blowing from, and understanding the pulse of consumer behaviour – you can build a plan based on what you need now, what you need next, and what your need later - without losing your core focus.

* *

At JGC – We help you pinpoint WHO you help, HOW you help, and WHY it matters. We are your full-service B2B Marketing Team.

* *

We all know that what worked before today may not work going forward – and vice versa. Knowing something needs to change is the easy part. Figuring out what that change is takes courage, time, and a willingness to fail – in order to thrive. When companies are not open to a much-needed change or become impatient waiting for it to make the desired impact, they often revert to "the way it's always been done," – thus beginning an insane loop of doing the same thing over and over, with hopes of a different outcome.

* *

We will help you think differently and show you data to consider alternatives - as we all know that what worked before may not work going forward.

* *

I do not believe in wasting dollars, resources, or time. If you don't know who you help, how you help, and why it matters, that's exactly what you're doing. Because without those answers, you'll be forever "throwing pasta at the wall to see what sticks." An effective marketing and lead-gen strategy cannot be formed without those answers, and it's my job to help you get them, with a razor-sharp focus on what you need most now – and limit time spent unnecessarily on what can wait for later.

Here are a few questions that get the ball rolling to help companies pinpoint their quickest time to money:

- What are you selling?

- To whom are you selling?

- Where are you making the most money?

- Where are you losing the most money?

- Who influences the decision to buy your product or service?

- Who are your top clients, and why?

- How did you find them?

- What was the client's *A-ha* moment that ultimately led to business?

- What's the LTV (lifetime value) of each customer?

- How much are you willing to invest in acquiring a new customer?

- What has been your most successful lead generation activity to date?

- What has been least successful?

- When visitors land on your website's home page, can they tell within the first 5 seconds who you help, how you help, and why it matters?

Think about it this way: if I handed you 100 leads right now – how would you choose the top 10?

- As the picture begins to paint itself, expand your palette by answering:

- What does your prospect-to-customer journey look like?

- How will you nurture prospects into qualified leads?

- How long is the average prospect-to-customer sales cycle?

- At what point does a prospect convert into a pipeline opportunity?

- Once the lead is handed off to sales, how prepared are they to run with it?

Then, if you dare, go back and answer "Why" for each.

Be honest. Be brutally honest. Your answers will result in your success – or ultimate failure.

* *

If I handed you 100 leads right now –
how would you choose the top 10?

* *

Here's a story of a salesman from a shoe-making company who went to an impoverished country where most people did not wear anything on their feet. He returned and reported that it is not a market they should focus on as no one wears shoes. Another new salesman went to the same market and came back smiling and excited. He reported that there's a market with enormous scope to educate people on the benefits of wearing something on their feet.

* *

Likewise, a printing company can print labels for the wine industry but fail to go after other industries looking for alternate packaging options. Whether it's producing interactive, engaging

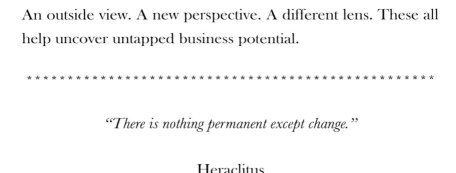

elements (like **QR** codes or **RFID** tags), digital embellishments that add a superior element of touch, or sustainable options that address consumer concerns – replicating what works and adapting it to a new market is a quicker time to money than starting from scratch.

An outside view. A new perspective. A different lens. These all help uncover untapped business potential.

* *

"There is nothing permanent except change."

Heraclitus

* *

Pareto's principle says, "80% of the consequences come from 20% of causes." This applies to many aspects, particularly Sales, where 80% of your revenue comes from 20% of your customers. When you know who makes up your top 20%, you can develop strategies to find and engage more just like them. By optimizing your resources, you can find, nurture, and convert more of the right prospects into pipeline opportunities.

Here's the thing, though. Not everyone is focused on driving leads as their marketing mandate. Instead, you might find yourself preparing for a merger or acquisition, seeking an **IPO**, launching a new product, building your brand, or planning your exit. I've experienced it all first-hand, and it's left me with an innate ability to holistically connect the right dots and appeal to the right investors, partners, influencers, journalists, or whoever you are targeting.

Operations may need a tweak, the sales team may need to learn new methods, your workflow may need adjustments, or you could be sitting on a goldmine of data without even realizing it.

I get it.

Connecting the dots requires a left-brain/right-brain combo – and that's the true value I bring to my team, to my clients, and now to you.

* *

If you always do what you always did, you'll always get what you always got.

* *

If you have deviated from your core and are meandering, now might be the right time to make a U-turn. If there's a habit of complacency, an inability to change course or make some tough decisions, here's what I have to say: If you always do what you always did, you'll always get what you always got.

* *

What can go wrong, will go wrong

"Be clear about your goal but be flexible about the process of achieving it."

- Brian Tracy

In a world where Murphy's Law reigns supreme, the phrase "what can go wrong will go wrong" holds an unwavering truth. Whether it's a meticulously planned event or a simple daily routine, unforeseen mishaps seem to lurk around every corner, ready to derail our best-laid plans.

How you bounce back is what matters the most.

Here's a case study on how my marketing team emerged victorious against all odds and obstacles, launching a new software solution at the 2005 Networld + Interop trade show in Las Vegas.

Company: BorderWare Technologies (acquired by WatchGuard in 2009)

Event: Networld+Interop 2005

Where: Las Vegas – Mandalay Bay

Purpose: Bring new software to market, build a database of prospects, media/influencers, and partners

Concept: Not only did we have a huge booth (if memory serves, it was 40 x 40), but we were also giving away a BMW Z30. It was parked in front of the Mandalay Bay convention centre in Las Vegas, with a guard and two booth agents (hired models and actors) representing us at all times.

The booth agents handed out high gloss postcards and entry forms for the draw scheduled at the show's end, which would be happening live from our booth. Their uniform consisted of form-fitting, one-piece pit crew jumpsuits, with the booth number emblazoned on the back of it.

As they walked the show floor, attendees would gravitate towards the bright blue and orange jumpsuits and follow them back to the booth, where we'd invite them to fill out a form and enter the draw to win the car. (no badge scanners back then!)

The booth was set to feature printed collateral, case studies, product spec sheets, and more. When it came time to set up, we were horrified to discover that NONE of it had arrived. Not one single piece.

Transferring files was arduous; file transfer protocol (FTP) sites were not yet commonplace. Plus, our graphic designer was on the East Coast while we were on the West. Time was not on our side.

We pulled an all-nighter, found a 24-hour Kinkos, managed to get the files transferred, and reproduced all the collateral – at the cost of $5000 USD. Today, that's the equivalent of $7500 USD (over $10,000 CAD).

The end did justify the means, however. We were the most talked-about booth at the show, and it was the most successful event in the company's history.

We added over 2500 contacts to our database and garnered an obscene amount of press.

The event resulted in hundreds of thousands of dollars in revenue (see attached testimonial)

And we gave away a freaking car!

I'll never forget the sleep-deprived laughter, camaraderie, and unwavering support of the team. We sang songs, cracked crazy jokes, and forged lifelong memories. To this day, I cannot think of Mandalay Bay without fond memories of "the green mile" between the hotel and the convention that we walked back and forth that long, crazy night back in 2005.

Oh... and the missing collateral? It arrived on the last day of the show. The boxes were all broken and held together with bright yellow tape, looking (appropriately) like a crime scene.

Seriously... you can't make this s*** up!

Imagine spending tens of thousands of dollars on a booth – only to sit there with nothing to back up your sales pitch, nothing to give away, and, most importantly, no way to capture leads! It was a disaster. But instead of panicking, we rallied together, rolled up our sleeves, and got to work.

We pulled it off, and it proved to be one of my biggest success stories. Yes, I thrived in the chaos. Again.

Opinions are like assholes – everybody has one

"Make it Simple
Make it memorable
Make it inviting to look at
Make it fun to read."

- Leo Burnett

Marketing is what gets people interested in your company's product or service. This happens through market research, analysis, and understanding who you help, how you help, and why it matters. Marketing impacts all aspects of a business, from sales to recruitment. At its core, awareness, and engagement is how B2B marketers are measured. Lead generation typically tops their KPI (Key Performance Indicator) list.

It's not about making noise about your product or service aimlessly but about making the right noise at the right place and for the right audience. To do that successfully takes skill, intuition, guts, curiosity, and Teflon skin. Because opinions are like assholes – everyone has one – especially when it comes to marketing!

When I started my career, we didn't have access to the massive amounts of data and insights we do today. We relied heavily on our guts, instincts, and experiences – backed by market research and customer feedback. Everyone had an opinion.

Customer experience plays a critical role in any company's success. Today, marketing is driven by technology, data, and predictive analytics combined with instincts, experience, and curiosity. Hoping to strike the perfect balance, marketers walk a constant tightrope between feelings and facts, psychology and numbers – left brain and right brain. And still, everyone has an opinion.

Research plays a crucial part in my work, as does asking the right questions. Open-ended, strategic questions that can't be answered by a simple yes or not. Questions that help you see the forest from the trees. While some may seem foolish or obvious, each answer plays a role in pinpointing your quickest time to money.

* *

It's not about making noise about your product or service aimlessly but about making the right noise at the right place and for the right audience.

* *

A corporate marketer needs leads to feed the sales pipeline, and their ability to convert a potentially off-target lead into one with pipeline potential happens by building and nurturing prospects throughout their buying journey. No lead is irrelevant.

Imagine you have a booth at a trade show. Will your success be based on the amount of traffic that comes to your booth? The number of badge scans? The amount of press coverage you get? The number of demos you give? Or the amount of qualified leads that came out of it?

This is where marketing and sales need to have their acts together, including agreement on how to triage leads, what the follow-up strategy is, and how it will be executed.

Defining all the various types of leads is crucial – here are a few that I have used over the years (in alphabetical order).

- Already a customer

- Analyst

- Candidate for hire

- Cold

- Competitor

- Consultant

- Former customer

- Hot

- Investor

- MQL/Marketing qualified lead (aka top of funnel/ nurture/marketing/prospect)

- Media/Influencer

- Partner/Vendor

- SQL/Sales qualified lead

- Warm

Tip: I don't recommend using "other." It's too easy to use as a dumping ground, and it will ultimately turn into a graveyard. Get as granular as you can.

Having agreement on the different lead types makes it easy to create your triage and follow-up strategy based on:

- Which leads require nurturing (marketing) and which require immediate contact (sales)

- Where they fit in the pipeline

- Where they add value to your business

Beware! Before you trigger a lead as bad, irrelevant, or (my personal pet peeve) dead, recognize the business potential that each brings. Then let marketing nurture those contacts and fine-tune the process along the way while garnering valuable insights like:

- What's the lifecycle of a lead?

- How many touches does it take to convert a prospect into a lead?

- At what part of the acquisition journey does that conversion take place?

- What triggers it?

- What is the average cost of a lead?

- What's our ROI?

Don't be quick to discredit the tire kickers. You know, the ones who come for the free pen. Even the most irrelevant leads hold potential because you don't know who they know – yet. It could be their father or uncle or cousin or neighbour, or even the parents of your children's friends. At some point, the conversation will turn to, "Do you know anyone who can help me [insert service here]?"

How much is it worth it for you and your company to be top of mind when that moment strikes - and they suddenly remember the t-shirt they got from that AWESOME company booth they visited?

Turning Setbacks into Success

"You can bring all the talent and say you're going to depend on that, but that only gets you so far. Every piston has to be hitting in the engine to win. You have to execute."

\- Bryan Larrison

The pandemic taught us how to do business in a virtual world. Building relationships and communicating with clients and partners became possible no matter where they were and shifted the conversation away from "we need you onsite" to "let's meet online."

While there are benefits to meeting physically, technology (and the pandemic) has helped us break all the walls. Today, I can see reactions on-screen – whether it's smiling faces, nodding heads, furrowed brows, or curious confusion – whether they are across the globe or across the street. Geography has become history.

Despite this, I still get asked, "How will you understand our product if you're not in the office?"

Here's the thing. You need to understand your product thoroughly. I need to know how to best market it. That means understanding your audience and why what you do matters to them. I can say that with authority because I've been there, I've done that, and I'm literally writing the book!

I've travelled the globe to take the pulse of the customer. I've been to the factories, showrooms, demo centres, innovation centres, labs, boardrooms, and press checks. I've produced tradeshows, conferences, customer appreciation events, and exhibitions; I understand what it takes to pull people to your booth with innovative ideas. I've implemented crazy ideas to increase booth traffic and generate leads. I've learned from failure and from success. I take all opinions into consideration.

* *

You need to understand your product thoroughly.
I need to know how to best market it.

* *

When it comes to business, I have high standards for myself and expect nothing less from the team, wherever they happen to be. If I'm the booth manager at a tradeshow, I lay down the law, whether you're the CEO, an intern, or have been schmoozing customers and prospects until 4 am and have a hangover. When you come to the booth, you come to work. Not to be on your phone. Not to take 45-minute bio breaks. And most definitely not to doze off in the corner.

Some would say I'm fearless because I'm not afraid to speak from the heart. Some would say I'm blunt because I say it like I see it. I'm instinctive; I'm restless and equally maverick. It's how I can connect dots that many don't see, spot untapped opportunities - and control the chaos.

It all starts with curiosity – and constantly peeling the why onion. In other words, no matter what the question is, keep asking why to the answer... until eventually you get to the real challenge at hand. Persistence and raw honesty are key.

No idea is bad unless not tried. In other words, we cannot be truly successful without learning from failure.

I've worked with a variety of people over the years and learned from them all, good and bad. That gave me an edge. I worked with product management, product marketing, public relations, investor relations, finance, HR, facilities, and the executive suite. At some point in time, somebody always needed Joanne to help them find, do or figure out something. I absorbed every experience like a sponge. Failure has led me to success every time.

Look at the Post-It example of 3M.

The adhesive formula was a mistake but became one of the greatest innovations in history.

Look at the Viagra story.

Pfizer originally developed the sildenafil compound to treat hypertension (high blood pressure) and angina pectoris (chest pain due to heart disease). During the heart clinical trials, researchers discovered that the drug was more effective at inducing an effect elsewhere than treating angina.

* *

I have earned the label of a curious marketer. Clients have understood I will try crazy things and suggest whacky ideas they are reluctant to test. Failure has led me to success every time.

* *

Once you balance conventional thinking with whacky ideas, can think on your feet, tweak, adapt, challenge, experiment, and willingly make mistakes – you can turn lemons into lemonade – and make it as a corporate marketer.

* *

Some would say I'm fearless because I'm not afraid to speak from the heart. Some would say I'm blunt because I say it like I see it. I'm instinctive; I'm restless and equally maverick. It's how I can connect dots that many don't see, spot untapped opportunities - and control the chaos.

* *

Roll up your sleeves
and figure it out

"I have no special talent. I'm only passionately curious."

- Albert Einstein

I have proudly earned the label of being a curious marketer. Clients expect me to try crazy things and suggest whacky ideas that they themselves are reluctant or unable to imagine. I get passionate and carried away, sometimes giving away more ideas than intended. But isn't that what you want from the person responsible for your brand?

No learned skill goes to waste, no matter how benign.

The great Steve Jobs learned calligraphy, which he used in designing the fonts he offered on his computers and laptops. In high school, I learned how to touch-type. Which means I can type fast. Really fast, especially when compared to my typesetting peers in college. What took them an hour to enter, I could get done in 10 minutes. Literally, with my eyes closed! I used that to my advantage to learn every nuance of the machine as I became the go-to person when large volumes of copy needed to be set. Needless to say, I became great at coding too.

When you start your career, you work to learn and then, over the years, work to earn.

I switched from being a graphic designer to working as an in-house corporate marketer for one of Canada's most successful software companies. Delrina, creators of PerForm, and FormFlow (to name a few), and most notably, WinFax PRO, which made it possible to fax from your computer. It was a game-changer - and my foray into the tech space. I had no clue what I was in for.

I remember being at a trade show demonstration, fascinated to see the presenter use his mouse and how, like magic, everything was flashed on a massive screen with throngs of people glued to the experience.

I was surrounded by computers everywhere, with no clue how to even power them on – let alone use a mouse! But on my first day, a colleague took pity on me and gave me a crash course on how to use that magical mouse, launch programs, and save files. But that was just the beginning.

Remember the whole left brain/right brain thing? Well, both sides were on fire, surrounded by all this new technology and potential. Before this, the only tech I'd worked with was a phototypesetter and stat camera – both of which have since been relegated to the museum of forgotten art supplies (www. forgottenartsupplies.com).

Hungry to learn and curious to try everything, I often stayed late. I made (a lot of) mistakes. I lost data. I lost entire files! But I never lost hope. I rolled up my sleeves and figured it out. Fast forward 30+ years, and my hunger to learn hacks, shortcuts, and new technology remains strong as ever.

Curiosity has yet to kill this cat!

What's your why?

"You really have to have a goal. The goal posts might shift but you should have a goal. Know what it is you need to find out."

- Zaha Hadid

When it comes to marketing, what you think you need is not always what you truly need. For example, when asked a generic inquiry like, "Do you do PR?" what's really being asked is, "Do you write press releases?" (We do both, by the way).

Faced with a litany of deliverables, it helps to see the big picture, think about how you will measure success, and what's driving your goals.

In other words, it all depends on your *why*.

When deliverables get lumped into the same category, it can result in a duplication of efforts, unnecessary spending, disjointed campaigns - and a lot of finger-pointing.

Here's a list of the programs (and deliverables) I'm usually asked about:

- **PR:** press releases, media relations, speaker's bureau, abstract pitches, and editorial calendars. Social Media: content creation, platform management, social selling, page management, training, and hashtag strategies.

- **Organic and/or Paid Search:** SEO, PPC, AdWords, Retargeting/Remarketing, keyword, and research.

- **Websites:** landing pages, optimization, CTAs (calls to action), redesign, and eCommerce/web-to-print.

- **Lead Generation:** CRM, workflow, automation, forms, tracking, and lead definitions.

- **Events** (trade shows, user groups, conferences, team building, branding, collateral, and swag.)

- Content development: Messaging playbooks, blogs, email campaigns, newsletters, landing pages, lead magnets, reels, and posts.

Recognizing the pain points driving your business decisions is a true *a-ha* moment. I love seeing the expression on people's face change as the lightbulb goes off in their heads – and they *get it*. From that moment on, they're hooked.

Getting to that moment takes a lot of onion peeling, as each answer to the question *why* reveals yet another layer to investigate.

My assessment of the client starts as soon as they are on my radar, before our first (virtual) meeting. I can get a good read on a company by looking at its website and its LinkedIn page.

- Website
  - Is the home page full of "We have, We do" statements?
  - When was the last time the site was updated?
  - Are there compelling calls to action?
  - How are leads collected?

* Is there content for all stages of the buyer journey – from "Just looking/I want to learn more" to "I'm ready to talk to a salesperson"

* Who works there?

- LinkedIn

  * Does the company page say the same thing as the website?

  * What can I learn about the exec team (anyone I know?)?

  * Is there an active brand? ambassador/spokesperson?

  * What type of content is being shared?

  * What level of engagement are they getting?

This helps me get a sense of where they're getting it right and where they could use some marketing help. More importantly, the questions I ask at this stage help them see what I see. I've learned through lots of trial and error (more error than trial) that for something to stick, you need to connect the dots yourself, with guidance – not conclusive statements – from someone who's *been there, done that.* This co-creation reduces friction points and is highly effective for both engagement and execution – and it's a lot more enjoyable too.

The *WHY* is the most important question you can ask or answer throughout the prospect-to-customer journey. The *how* and the *what* come later. And yes, you need to be able to answer those too.

Let's revisit the question, "Do you do PR?" (public relations) and look at how to peel back the onion and expose the *a-ha* moment by asking questions like:

- Why do you think PR is the most suitable solution?

- What does PR mean to you?

- How will it help you?

- How do you currently manage your PR needs?

- How will/do you measure success?

- Have you considered anything else to meet the same objectives?

- If yes, what are the other options?

- If no, why not?

The more you dig deep into each inquiry, the more you ask *why* or *why not,* and the harder it gets to answer each question, the clearer it gets to where the real problem lies – and what's needed most now, next, and later.

* *

*The **WHY** is the most important question you can ask -or answer -*
throughout the prospect-to-customer journey.

*The **how** and the **what** come later.*

And yes, you need to be able to answer those too.

* *

One of the first questions I ask companies looking for more leads is, "how are you collecting, storing, and managing your leads today?" In other words, what CRM are you running?

The answer to that one question alone impacts any lead gen strategy and focuses us to pinpoint what's needed now from what's needed later.

Here again, asking the right questions is what we do best.

How to stretch your time – and money

*"Either you run the day
or the day runs you."*

- Jim Rohn

Have you ever had one of those polarizing moments – when everything that needs to get done swirls around in your head and makes you feel like Dorothy in the Wizard of Oz? It's that feeling when you realize you have so much to get done – but you have absolutely no idea where to start.

In an Express Employment Professionals survey of more than 18,000 business leaders, 57% of respondents said they lose six work hours per week due to disorganization. Disorganized employees who make $50,000 annually cost their companies about $11,000 per year in lost time due to their disorganization.

No matter what business you're in, no matter what role you play, and no matter how old you are, there's always something being added to your to-do list. Here are six proven ways to get organized – and stretch your time (and money).

1 – Organize your desk:

For me, the best way to be productive is to have everything in sight. But if that results in you wasting time rummaging for things regularly, it's time to sort through the chaos that is your desk.

Not to be confused with a barren desk, having an organized desk means that you can find what you need quickly when you need it. After all, according to Researchers at the University of Minnesota, a messy desk is a sign of genius!

I once worked for a company that had a strict clean desk policy that nearly broke me. Thankfully, I've learned how to adapt the concept of a clean desk with one that suits the genius in me – and ensures a clean desk at the end of the day – and a clean desk at the start.

2 – Make lists:

Making a list isn't all that difficult. Managing it – that's a whole other ball game. I like Google Tasks, but I still prefer my 3×5, lined sticky notes to capture my sparks of genius (or a to-do I completely forgot about) when I'm at my desk. Having a notebook for to-dos as I think of them – to be crossed off as they are either completed, delegated, or moved to a calendar – is liberating. So is crumpling up and tossing that post-it!

There's no shortage of task management software. Take advantage of free trials and figure out what combination of high-tech and low-tech solutions works for you.

3 – Use your calendar:

Once you have a clear picture of what needs to get done, you can properly plan out when – and how – it will happen. Use your calendar to schedule your time and stick to it. Tasks with hard due dates go in first, around any scheduled appointments or meetings. Travel time? Schedule it. But leave some breathing room, or you will have no options when something new gets added to the mix – sending you spiraling back to Oz.

When I started booking my personal and family to-dos into my Gmail calendar and my company to-dos in my business calendar, my stress level went way down. This gives a clear view of what must get done and when – and if any potential conflicts are getting in the way.

4 – Tackle the procrastination monster:

Schedule brain breaks based on how long you can go before becoming distracted – whether every 20 minutes or every 2 hours. Use the time to get up, stretch, get some fresh air, and clear your mind. Schedule your distractions: when you will check social media when you'll check email when you'll return phone calls – and when you will be working on tasks.

5 – Embrace the power of subject lines:

Management consulting firm, McKinsey & Company, reports that the average worker spends 28% of their work week on email. That's more than 11 hours a week.

Often overlooked is the subject line's ability to get to the point. Quickly. Need a reply by Friday? Put it in the subject line. Need a question answered? Subject: Answer needed for highlighted question in the body of the email by Thursday. Don't forget to highlight the question!

The best part is that you can change the subject line as the email thread progresses – or even changes direction – from the original.

6 – Be kind to yourself:

Life happens – and there will be days when your schedule is thrown completely out of whack. That's when you need to take a deep breath, roll up your sleeves and reset. While it may be painful at first, using these strategies will help you get s*** done – and give you the mindset to focus on business, family, friends – and yourself.

* *

In the world of marketing, delivering *yesterday* is the norm. There's always something happening at the last minute, and the deadlines can seem absurd and crazy, but as we all know, what can go wrong, will go wrong. All you can do is take it in stride while you roll up your sleeves and just get it done.

Be like a duck. Stay calm on the surface but paddle like hell underneath.

Here are the aspects crucial for productive multi-taking:

- *Know what's driving the dates and the deadlines.* Focus first on hard, immovable dates that simply cannot be moved – like the early bird deadline for shipping your trade show booth and materials. Miss that, and you start cutting into your ROI (Return on Investment).

- *Don't go for perfection always.* Steve Jobs famously said, "Real artists ship." He was referring to the fact that everyone has ideas, but real artists deliver on them – or ship them, as he put it.

Creative thinking can lead to amazing things, but only if you do something with it. The idea you never implement will not help you or anyone else. It can't. To have any impact on anything, your creativity needs to see the light of day. You need to put it out there for it to have wings and take off. You need to ship it.

- *Work Backwards.* Working backward with the end in mind works brilliantly. Without an end date, there will always be something more important – and there will always be something unfinished.

- Breaking the tasks into short, bite-sized goals is something I practice a lot. The sense of accomplishment is a positively joyous experience and provides motivation to keep moving forward.

- I've already mentioned Calendaring, which helps you focus more on the immediate tasks. Beware of over-calendaring and be mindful of scheduling breaks.

- Find your fuel. Music plays an important role and fuels both sides of my brain. When working with words, soft instrumental music keeps me focused. When dealing with numbers and spreadsheets, the volume goes up. When I need the creative juices to flow, the music is loud and full of energy. Much like a foodie cleanses their palette between courses, music helps me reset and re-focus my brain as it shifts between left and right.

* *

In the world of marketing, delivering "yesterday" is the norm.
There's always something happening at the last minute,
and the deadlines can seem absurd and crazy,
but as we all know, what can go wrong, will go wrong.
All you can do is take it in stride, roll up your sleeves,
and just get it done.
Be like a duck.
Stay calm on the surface but paddle like hell underneath.

* *

The significance of one-twenty-one (121)

"Don't miss the synchronicity of what is happening right now finding its way to your life at just this moment. There are no coincidences in the universe, only convergences of Will, Intent and Experience."

- Neal Donald Walsch

It was a cold morning, and I woke up to my alarm. I took a few steps, brushed my teeth, and headed to the kitchen for my morning tea. I glanced at my fitness app and thought to myself, "Here we go," as the number of steps taken came into view. Later, as I glanced at my watch, there it was again. I booked an Uber – and it was there, too, right on the license plate. I found a receipt in my wallet – and the unbelievable happened again. Finally, after a long, hard day,

I was ready to relax and watch something on TV. When I hit the pause button, I chuckled at the timestamp. Right there. Staring me straight in the face. The number 121 appeared in its glory. Again and again and again.

* * * * * * * * * * * * * * * *

Have you ever come across a number, a sign, or a message that repeatedly presents itself - in the oddest places, at the strangest times, and in the most random forms? It can be absolutely anything that keeps showing up in your personal or professional life.

121 (one-twenty-one) is one of those random numbers that really is not quite so random in my life, mysteriously appearing on receipts, tickets, clocks, registers, signs – anywhere numbers appear.

As with most aspects of my life, rather than fight it, I have chosen to embrace it.

Shocking as this seems, I am NOT the only Joanne Gore on the internet! The domain JoanneGore.com was taken when I went to buy it. So, what better way to quickly distinguish myself from the other Joanne Gores out in the world? It was time to put my magic number to work.

The first website I launched was JoanneGore121.com – long before Joanne Gore Communications. To this day, many of my online profiles include the number 121, including my LinkedIn and Twitter profiles, both JoanneGore121.

A coincidence is a seemingly random or unexpected event or series of events that appear related but may not be caused by any direct connection. Coincidences can be surprising and sometimes seem mysterious or meaningful, but they are ultimately just the result of chance.

There are many different types of coincidences, and they can occur in a variety of contexts. Some people believe that coincidences are signs or messages from the universe or a higher power, while others view them simply as random events with no deeper meaning. No scientific evidence supports the idea that coincidences have any special significance – and yet they can still be exciting and fascinating to think about.

Your life is shaped by the choices you make.

I have come across this situation very often. Tickets, receipts, clocks, time stamps, the bar code on grocery receipts, the number of steps I've taken, distances, prices – you name it.

121 is always there.

Each time it happens, I take pause. Is it a sign? What does it mean? What is it trying to tell me? Not every instance has merit - and gets chalked up as yet one more *coincidence*. I barely blink anymore when 1:21 shows up as the time of day. But collectively, it's so much more than that. Collectively, it's about the daily patterns and habits that shape our life – and the life-changing signs that impact our journey.

In business, nothing is more powerful than a one-to-one (1-2-1) meeting to foster relationships and nurture growth. The numeric co-relation is not lost on me. Has this been my calling all along?

The point I'm trying to make is that this number holds some special place in my life, and every time I connect the dots and uncover a new meaning, it has worked favourably for me. Did I mention that my birthday is *January 21st*, aka 1/21?

The universe speaks to us through signs. It's up to us to recognize them.

Have you experienced a situation where you are about to make a decision, but you're conflicted? Has the voice inside you ever said, "Hey! Stop, think it over, take a pause – just wait." Have your spidey senses ever tingled just as you're about to make a decision or commit to something?

Those are the moments where, with open eyes, these signs appear to guide you.

What's your "121"?

* *

The universe speaks to us through signs. It's up to us to recognize them.

* *

When the world experienced the traumatic and crippling Coronavirus pandemic between 2019 and 2022, it brought everything to a standstill. In 2023, when this book was written, its persistence remains an ongoing global threat.

My business revolves around people, and seeing how they react to ideas, results, and analysis is critical to mutual success. Phone conversations simply don't cut it, nor will lengthy emails – which, at best, would be merely skimmed. I want to see my client's smile, their head nodding in agreement or even shaking in disbelief – as we pinpoint their quickest time to money.

* *

There is nothing more powerful than the simplicity of a smile.

* *

I'm very expressive. Anyone who has ever had a conversation with me will attest; my body language conveys much more than my words. In turn, client (and prospect) conversations are more meaningful – and memorable.

COVID forced us online and opened new opportunities to do business - via video. For me, it was a complete game-changer, further cementing the significance of the numbers: one-two-one and one-twenty-one.

Somewhere 121 has become deeply rooted in my subconsciousness. Dr. Joseph Murphy writes in his influential book *The Power of Subconscious Mind* that we have two minds – one conscious mind and the other subconscious. The latter works non-stop, even when we sleep, and the book explains how we can use the subconscious mind to influence our habits and choices toward any situation or person.

Next time your *121* shows itself, make a conscious note of it, and let it embrace you as you seek its significance. For me, it was a number, but it could have been a colour, a scent, a type of car, a name - literally anything that is an undeniably, not-so-random yet random, presence in your life.

Here's a (very small) glimpse of my 121 collections:

121 – coming announcement

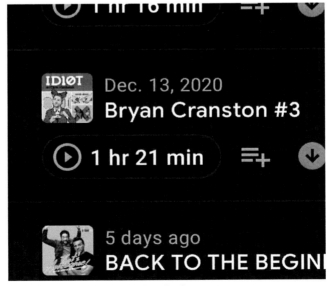

121 Podcast

The daughter of hockey star Tim Horton has retired as a franchisee in the coffee chain that bears his name, urging her peers to "keep demanding better" as declining profitability has led to tensions with parent company Restaurant Brands International Inc.

QSR-T +1.21% ▲

Article with 121

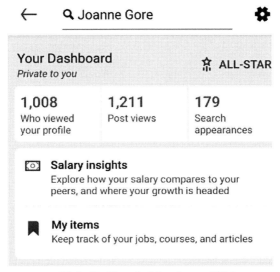

LinkedIn Post Article views -1211

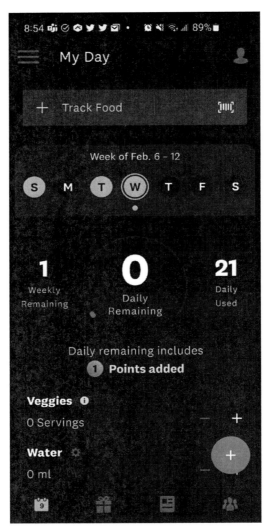

Food Tracker 1 21

Best Fiends Game goals– 121

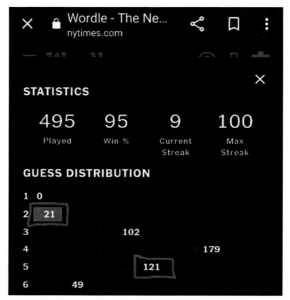

Screenshot

Walmart Product Reference POS

Quantity	Total
1	$16.99

Ground : Free
Shipped on 09/17/2020
Tracking# 1Z68V4842013033996

McCafé Premium
Roast Coffee, 1.36 kg
Item #1212212
$21.99

2-Day Delivery

Quantity	Total
2	$43.98

Ground : Free
Shipped on 09/17/2020
Tracking# 1Z68V4842013033996

Order Summary

Subtotal (5 Items)	$88.95
Shipping & Handling	$0.00
GST (G)	$0.00

Product Order No. 1212212

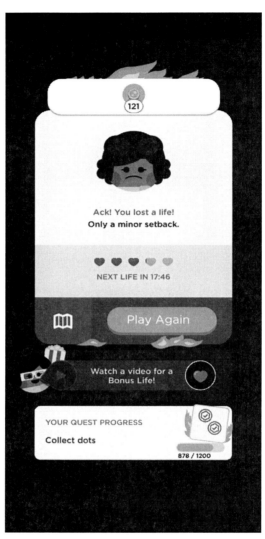

Two Dots game – 121 Coins

this month.

The Crown corporation confirmed Wednesday that there had been 121 cases at its Dixie Road location.

News Article – 121 cases

Opening Credits of a TV Show

Channelling your passion: Lessons learned from the fitness industry

"Strength does not come from winning.
Your struggles develop your strengths. When you go through hardships
and decide not to surrender, that is strength."

\- Arnold Schwarzenegger

My battle with the scale started at home. My grandmother and my mother often used to argue about the way I dressed. It was the early 70s. Patterns were bold, and the cuts were loose and flowing. My grandmother always felt that the clothes I chose made me look fat. Today, we'd call it body *shaming*. But when I was 8, that term didn't exist, and the lifelong scars those conversations caused were yet unknown.

Gym class was a horrific experience for me. I was a short, fat, weak girl, laughed at and ridiculed. The thought of exercise, fitness, running, and jogging fuelled anxiety.

When I started high school, cliques were formed, and I was labelled a nerd. Childhood friends became overnight bullies. If you've ever seen a John Hughes movie, I embodied the outcast cliché.

My parents separated when I was 8. From the ages of 8 to 12, my grandmother lived with us while my mother returned to work as a legal secretary. Born in Romania, she was a phenomenal cook and baker. Having lived through two world wars, she had seen it all.

Corn remains Romania's top grain crop in terms of area and production, followed by wheat and barley. Romania is Europe's largest sunflower producer and a top three producer of corn, wheat, and soybeans. It was always a treat to watch her cook and serve us home-cooked stews, cornbread (mamaliga), beet soup (borscht), strudel (from scratch), sweet and savoury noodle puddings (kugel), potato dumplings (varenekas), and hamburgers (cucklettes) – to name a few.

Not being wasteful came second nature to her; I learned the art of frugality at an early age. I adopted this trait throughout my personal life and professional career – always making the most of the resources at hand. This attitude has served me well when developing (and defending) budgets.

Working hand-in-hand with CFOs, CEOs, and business owners, I've learned that no matter the size of the marketing spend, every penny serves a purpose. If you can't justify the spend, it could end up on the chopping block at any time.

The truth is – whether you're managing a budget of fifty thousand dollars or five million dollars – your success boils down to one thing and one thing only:

Why?

It doesn't matter if you're a scrappy startup or an established enterprise – you need KPIs to measure your ROI (Return on Investment). In other words, you need to know:

- Why are we spending the money?
- How will it impact our goals?
- How will we measure results?

* *

The truth is — whether you're managing a budget of fifty thousand dollars or five million dollars — your success boils down to one thing and one thing only:

Why?

* *

Back to my story.

I was in a new city, starting a new career, with none of my childhood friends around for support. We communicated over telephone landlines, and through physical mail.

It was the mid-eighties and another ten years before the dawn of the home PC. Little did I know at the time that I would be part of the team that would launch the Compaq Presario to Canadian consumers in the mid-nineties,

But I digress.

My roommate encouraged me to join the JCC (Jewish Community Centre). Aerobics was in its heyday, and the JCC was a great place to meet my peers – many also hailing from Montreal. There was only one catch.

It was a community FITNESS centre!

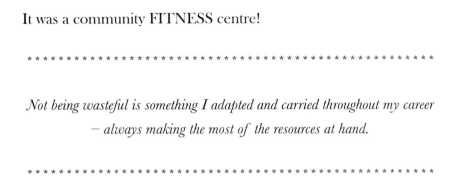

* *

Not being wasteful is something I adapted and carried throughout my career – always making the most of the resources at hand.

* *

Nonetheless, I sucked it up, put on a brave face, and began my fitness journey. At first, I looked at it purely as a social activity. I started participating in classes, making friends, and socializing.

Fitness was no longer the enemy. I discovered a whole new passion and immersed myself in the world of aerobics. The music, the energy in the room, the routines – both sides of my brain were firing on all cylinders.

In my quest to know the "why" in everything, I took more and more of an interest, attended classes in different clubs, and learned from a variety of instructors. When I discovered that the JCC offered a fitness instructor course, I jumped at the chance to learn all I could about the science behind the effort. I was seeing a lot of instructors (and participants) getting injured – and it really nagged at me.

I figured if I could understand the why, I could modify any exercise or routine to suit my own capabilities, as well as help others.

I was hooked. In 1988 I became an aerobics instructor. In 1995, the Association for Canadian Fitness Professionals (CanFitPro) launched the Fitness Instructor Specialist (FIS) certification; I was amongst the first wave of instructors to become certified in Canada. To this day, I volunteer my time behind the scenes as a team leader at their annual national fitness conference in Toronto.

I was working out regularly, had an active circle of friends, had free access to gyms all around Toronto – and I was getting paid! I had transitioned from an unhealthy, overweight girl into a fitness fan.

Interestingly, even when I was pregnant, I continued working out (safely), teaching step classes until my eighth month, stopping only because I had to keep running to the bathroom! For once – the focus of my large size was not shameful. I was proud to encourage and motivate people of all fitness levels to move.

I had a caesarean with all three children. For about six weeks post-pregnancy, I was limited in the activity I was permitted. No lifting, no driving standard, no jumping, and absolutely no aerobics!

So, I turned lemons into lemonade and formed a *mommy and me* group of new mothers. We'd get together and do gentle activities with our babies to stay fit, stay cheerful, and stay sane. Weight Watchers helped me shed the pregnancy pounds, and I returned after each birth.

Me being me – I wanted to share all I'd learned to achieve and maintain my lifelong goal. I joined the company in 2013 as a group leader and wellness coach.

Everything changed in March 2020 when the COVID-19 pandemic forced us into lockdown. WW meetings went online almost immediately – but not without early adopter glitches. Members were scared. We were scared. We all were doing our best.

In Canada, the health and fitness industry was hit hard. For the better part of 2 years, gyms were shut down, as were most WW centres. Memberships dropped. Locations closed. There were layoffs – and more layoffs. I was furloughed and eventually terminated.

I no longer had anything holding me accountable to my health. Fitness went out the window. I tried Zoom classes, but they simply didn't do it for me.

So, I walked.

Walking is a simple yet powerful way to improve your physical and mental health. It can help reduce stress, clear your mind, and even boost creativity. Walking has many benefits, including improving concentration and memory, reducing the risk of depression, and helping to keep your heart healthy. Additionally, walking can help you to stay in shape by burning calories and strengthening muscles. Regular walks can improve your overall well-being by connecting with nature or spending quality time with friends or family.

But it wasn't enough.

Lack of exercise, being glued to the computer, online shopping, stress-eating, you name it - I lost my motivation. I forgot my *why*. My healthy mindset wavered, and I succumbed to old eating habits and unhealthy choices.

Two years later, I couldn't believe it when I saw my former self in the mirror – the one I had worked so hard to shed.

I knew it was time to reframe my thought process. While I could not control what was happening around me, I could control how I chose to feed my body, my mind, and my soul.

I set a BHAG (big hairy ass goal) to lose the Covid weight and get back in shape, despite an aging body, a back injury, a bad knee, and a global pandemic. And I set milestones to keep me motivated along the way. I discovered Pilates – a complete workout that not only mirrors physiotherapy exercises I've been treated with over the years but fires up muscles I didn't even know I had.

In January 2023, I crushed that BHAG - just 2 weeks shy of my birthday.

So why have I devoted an entire chapter to fitness? And what in the world does it have to do with B2B marketing?

Being a fitness leader and health & wellness coach helped me to pinpoint obstacles, reframe mindsets, and develop strategies that put you back in the driver's seat. When looked at through a business lens, that means:

- Always be learning. First and foremost, accept that setbacks happen. Use them as learning opportunities and figure out how to mitigate them in the future.

- Don't let others control your destiny. Whether I was teaching aerobics or leading a WW meeting, I helped people set their own goals and achieve their own success. I was there to provide support, ask tough questions, and offer options and strategies that could be adapted to any level or situation. I work the same way with my clients.

- Be an active listener. When you listen to hear instead of listening to speak, you can start connecting dots as you get a glimpse into how the other person thinks, feels, and responds to situations. This arms you with valuable insights when the need arises.

- Be kind to yourself. Treat yourself to what brings you joy, whether it's an ice cream cone, a walk in the park, or a round of golf. Reframe *cheat days* into *treat days*. Own your choices. Enjoy them. Celebrate them. But if your choices make you feel bad, or have negative ramifications, consider a different option next time.

- Life is full of U-turns. The world doesn't come to an end when you make a mistake. If you have a piece of cake, skip a workout, or choose french fries over salad, all is not lost. But when one slice turns into a whole pie, and you haven't gotten off the couch in a week – it becomes harder and harder to get back on track. Similarly, when companies make mistakes, it's essential to recognize them early and set them right before it gets past the point of no return.

- Bite the bullet, face your worst fears, and get your feet dirty. Skipping out on workouts (or skipping out on meetings) signals that you're not committed to doing what's necessary to hit your goals. When that happens, it's time to re-evaluate your objectives – and your strategy.

- Smile. There is nothing more powerful than the simplicity of a smile. I used to tell people coming to my classes to smile, laugh and have fun. It didn't matter if they were going left, and I was going right (as long as nobody got hurt!). As long as they remembered to breathe – and get out of their own head.

- Ask the right questions. There's a big difference between: "How much weight do you want to lose?" and "Why do you want to lose weight?" The same holds for business. "How many leads do you need?" is hardly the same as "What is the DNA of a lead?"

- Stay true to yourself. Ethics, discipline, morals, and process is a way of life, whether in fitness or your business. Consistency gets results.

- Be patient. Change doesn't happen overnight, but with passion and a hunger to excel, change does happen. Little by little, incremental changes in your body (or your business) will shine through as you target new milestones.

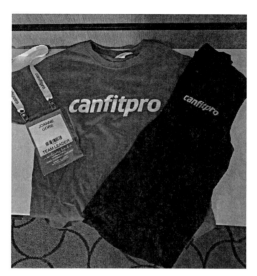

Can fit pro Team Leader Uniform

Can fit pro Team Leader Volunteer

Embrace chance. Embrace choice. Embrace the chaos.

... a peek inside a mind that thrives in chaos

"Life is not a problem to be solved, but a reality to be experienced."

- Neal Donald Walsch

How can you explain the unexplainable? It is a question that has been asked for centuries and has puzzled many of the greatest minds in history. These phenomena cannot be explained by science or mathematics, despite any evidence or aftereffects – all you can do is sit back and accept.

There have been a few key turning points in my life thus far that made me who I am today. I often play the "what-if" game, wondering how much of an impact these life events truly had. Would I have wound up the passionate, fierce B2B marketer I am today without them? How did they affect the decisions I've made since? How much of what happens to us is by choice? How much by chance?

Call it fate, divine intervention, luck, destiny, karma... whatever. I often wonder, did I make that choice - or was it some higher power guiding and shaping my future?

Some things are unexplainable.

* *

It was the year 1965, and a car was travelling on the highway from Montreal, Quebec, to a small town in the Laurentians, less than 100km (about 60 miles) north. There were no other cars on the road. Or so it seemed.

There were no seatbelt or child seat laws at the time; child safety wasn't much of a consideration before the early 70s. The toll roads did not have security cameras or today's scanning capabilities. In 1965, you had to slow down, roll down your window (by hand), throw in some change (hope it made it in!), and merge back into traffic.

There was a lady at the wheel, a nurse sitting next to her with a baby on her lap, and a boy sitting behind in the back seat. Somewhere near St. Jerome, shortly after clearing a toll, the mother lost control of the vehicle. In the following moments, the car veered off the shoulder of the road, flipped a few times, and landed in a ditch at the side of the road.

With my dad a few weeks before the accident.

I was the baby in that car - and I was six months old.

The nurse sitting next to my mother, the one holding me, feared I'd be propelled through the front windshield and threw me backward – and I rolled under the seat from which I had been thrown.

As fate would have it, another car was on the road that day. A police cruiser had been ahead of us both before and after we passed through the toll. When the officer checked his rear-view mirror and didn't see the car that had been behind him, he grew suspicious. There had been no exits between the toll booth to where he was – and he doubled back to see what had happened.

From the moment he found us to the time the ambulance arrived, my mother shouted, "My baby! My baby!" It was then that they found me under the seat. But that wasn't the end of it. Somehow, I had managed to chomp down on my tongue and sever it. And it needed to be found.

We were rushed to the nearest hospital, and I was separated from my family.

My mother had sustained broken arms, damage to her eye socket, and an assortment of physical (and psychological) injuries. They later resurfaced in the form of debilitating migraines and spinal trauma - leaving her bedridden with chronic back pain in the final years before her death.

The nurse suffered a broken leg, and my brother, as my mother loved to recant, "He just sat in the back seat reading his comic book. Unphased." Miraculously, he was untouched.

Shortly before the accident with my brother.

I heard this story told by my mother countless times before she passed. It still sends shivers up my spine.

And me? In addition to the severed tongue, which they found and re-attached, my legs and hips had been broken. It was uncertain whether I would ever walk – or talk.

I was six months old and already proving the world wrong.

* *

It was 1976/77. I was in Grade Seven (around eleven or twelve years old) when something strange happened. Something that propelled my fascination with words and language to a whole new level. Something that, to this day, cannot be explained.

I was a voracious reader even then, and my mother found it tough to match my pace as I consumed book after book. A friend had given us the entire library of Nancy Drew hardcover books. I would read 2 or 3 daily.

I am forever playing with words in my head. I love dissecting words, creating new words out of them, re-arranging syllables – playing with language.

French Immersion had recently been introduced into public schools so English Montrealers could obtain their bilingual certificate from the Government of Quebec. For those like me, too old to enter the track in Grade One, we could spend our final year of elementary school (Grade Seven) immersed in the French language all day. That meant every subject besides English was taught in French.

We spoke French at all times – in the playground, hallways, and at lunch. It was truly an immersive experience. And I am forever grateful I embraced the opportunity to attend. Knowing how to communicate in more than one language has served me well throughout my career. I encourage everyone to seize that opportunity.

On that fateful day in Grade Seven, I woke up and got ready to go to school. I'm not really sure when I realized it, but suddenly, I was able to speak backward. I mean literally backward. It sounds as crazy now as it did all those decades ago.

I eagerly showed off my new *foreign language* to my friends. Everyone tried to stump me, but it was tough. It didn't matter what word was thrown at me or in what language because I was able to see it. Phonetically. All I had to do was read it aloud. Backward.

Over the years, my ability to speak backward has been a great icebreaker. Who doesn't want to hear what their name is backward? My fascination with language and words evolved into a passion for typography, typographic design, spotting mistakes, and assessing the flow - and psychology - of finely crafted content and copywriting.

My colleagues, clients, and team know that if there's anything wrong to be found on the copy and content, I'm their go-to person. I will play the devil's advocate, seek out errors, and point out any messages that could lead to negative bombshells.

Perhaps it was because I was immersed in French all day long. Perhaps it was because my grandmother (who was living with us) mainly spoke Yiddish (a German derivative) at home. Was my fascination with language a choice? Or was chance, once again, guiding my way?

A few things are unexplainable.

* *

I would come home from school beaming with pride after receiving a particularly good grade. It didn't matter what it was; my mother would be thrilled and brag about how well I did. There was just one tiny thing. The grade was always slightly inflated – because good was never quite good enough. An 85%

(the equivalent of an A) on an exam became a 90%. A 90 became a 95. A 95 became 98.

I was a strong academic student. I got high grades, made the honour roll, won awards, skipped grades - and was constantly challenged to do better. Did that mess me up? Probably, yes. Did it drive me outside my comfort zone? Probably, yes. Is it why I am always filled with ideas to do more, make more – and help more? Most definitely, yes.

You can say I push myself a lot, which rubs off on my team and my work.

In today's competitive world, good is not enough to sustain long-term growth – both personally and professionally. We need to strive for excellence in all aspects of our lives. This means going beyond the basics and pushing ourselves to achieve goals that may seem impossible.

Conquering what seems impossible can be life-altering. It can give you the edge you need to stand out from the crowd, make a lasting impression, and help those around you. We must never forget that good is just the starting point, and excellence should be our ultimate goal.

But you know what I have learned in my quest for excellence?

It's that there is a time and a place for *good enough*." More importantly, I've learned how to prioritize what needs to be done now, what needs to happen next, and what can wait until later.

To do that, you need to figure out what your relationships, your job, your grades, your career, your health, your wealth - your responsibilities – are worth to you. If something is worth 60% of your effort, then aim for 70, accept 60, take the win, and move on to the stuff that actually requires 100% of your time.

Make every minute count.

Before Covid, I strove for 80 - 90% as my good to go benchmark – especially when the last 20% impacted valuable time to market. I've seen too many companies, both large and small, waste precious time agonizing over minutiae that could have easily been updated after going live. Instead, by the time they were happy, they'd lost their competitive advantage and their market share.

Post-pandemic, I'm seeing that drop to between 60% and 70%, with the impact of machine-learning solutions such as ChatGPT creating invisible benchmarks between good and great.

* *

Taming the Chaos

I thrive in the chaos. To me, anything less is boring. Once I recognized that, I learned how to channel its energy into positive productivity. For me, cleaning my desk has come to symbolize a fresh start after the chaos has been tamed. I embrace this cleansing ritual and its ability to instil calm and clarity. Knowing what comes next makes it possible to do what needs to be done now.

Finding patterns is another way to tame the chaos. My love for colours was not just because of what they look like but also for the rhythms, patterns, and synergy they provide.

My fascination with colours started at an early age – I remember organizing my crayons based on their hue as early as eight years old. In college, we studied colour psychology, and my fascination grew. We recreated colour wheels, chromatic grey scales, shades, and tints. It quickly became one of my favourite courses, alongside hand lettering and typesetting – firing all my left and right brain cylinders.

Find clarity and tame the chaos.

* *

Perfectionism vs. Procrastination? Chicken or Egg?

A therapist once told me, "There's nothing wrong with you. It's just that you are a perfectionist".

I wasn't sure if that was an insult or a compliment.

Perfectionists are known to have an all-or-nothing attitude, striving for excellence in all aspects of their life. They often set extremely high standards for themselves and are highly critical of their work. Perfectionists can be easily identified by their meticulous attention to detail and the extreme lengths they go to ensure that everything is perfect. They tend to be very organized and can often be seen taking extra steps to meet their expectations. Perfectionists may also pressure themselves and others as they strive for perfection. Yup. Spot on.

I don't accept mediocrity. I equate it with being lazy and unmotivated. But there's a difference between being mediocre and doing your best – whatever YOUR best looks like.

Research has proven a direct correlation between perfectionism and procrastination. If you think you fall into either of these two camps, you get it. You get why leaving something until the last minute gives you less time to agonize over its perfection.

To the outsider, my desk may seem completely disorganized. But I know exactly where everything is that I need – and it's all based on priority. Chances are, if you're a procrastinator like me, you also have a messy desk. But once you decide to clear it, the perfectionist in you comes out until it's immaculate, and you're ready to tackle what comes next. Lather, rinse, repeat. Which characteristic drives the other? Does it matter?

Learn to accept the unexplained.

* *

You're fired!
… now what?

"Trust the Wait.

Embrace the uncertainty. Enjoy the beauty of becoming.

When nothing is certain, anything is possible."

- Mandy Hale

Three short years following the pandemic of 2020, the technology upon which businesses, schools, and families became dependent has already been displaced.

"Zoom Joins Tech Giants in Announcing Layoffs"

In February of 2023, the New York Times reported that Eric Yuan, CEO of Zoom, announced the layoff of nearly 1,300 employees, the equivalent of 15% of its workforce. Microsoft, Alphabet, Salesforce, Meta, Amazon, and PayPal have also reduced their workforces.

Even Walt Disney Company, the mass media and entertainment conglomerate, lost its lustre – and its market share.

Entrepreneur.com reported how "Disney Plans to Fire 7000 Employees."

The layoff decision was announced right after the company announced quarterly earnings, while they also revealed its plan to reorganize the work structure and slash jobs to reduce cost."

* *

These announcements have become increasingly the norm, but they represent a business reality that's decades old. And the sad truth is that there's a lot more that doesn't make the news – than does.

With so much at risk, it's easy to question what goes on behind the scenes. How did it get so bad? How did it come to such extreme measures? Where was the writing on the wall?

Were there warnings of the storm ahead?

Yes.

Before the public announcements, there were private conversations. The closed-door meetings. The flurry of emails. The crisis management specialists. The PR team. The HR and legal teams. The scrutiny of expenses. The new faces. And the dreaded manilla envelopes.

I remember the first time I got fired. The walk to the bus stop, just a few yards away, was the longest walk I'd ever taken. I was sobbing; my emotions were uncontrollable. A colleague of mine drove past and offered a lift, but I chose to be left alone. I thought about how I'd manage expenses, pay the rent, and how long it would take to find a new job. Would I have to move back home? I wasn't prepared for this. I never dreamed this would happen to me. I was good at my job. I received high praise. Clients and colleagues loved me – and I them. But unbeknownst to me, the company wasn't thriving and had to lay people off.

I was one of the chosen.

* *

I remember the first time I got fired. The walk to the bus stop just a few yards away was the longest walk I'd taken. I was sobbing;

my emotions were uncontrollable. A colleague of mine drove past and offered a lift, but I chose to be left alone.

* *

I soon realized I was blessed with a strong support system of family and friends who had my back. If you're blessed to have these people in your life, you know that they love you unconditionally, not for what you have but for what you are. Seek them out. Keep them in your orbit.

I had moments of grief but didn't allow it to consume me. Not one to wait for things to happen, I knew I had to roll up my sleeves and move on. It was my stepmother who found me a job at the Kwik Kopy Printing located in her office building at 121 Bloor Street in Toronto. I s*** you not.

I was doing everything there - typesetting, designing, preparing layouts, meeting clients, taking creative briefs – I even ran the press in a pinch. I loved everything in this job except for Sales. I tried. It wasn't for me—at least not in those days of door-to-door print peddling.

Throughout my career, I've been terminated many times, in many ways, in myriad acquisitions and mergers. On rare occasions, I was spared; in most instances, I was that crossed-out line item on a spreadsheet. In retrospect, I now see the patterns and the warning signs that would have saved me tremendous grief and anxiety.

My employment with Brightspark, a technology incubator, was a huge eye-opener. It was the early 2000s and the era of the dot-com bubble. As part of the marketing team, our job was to launch software and technology startups and then help them either go public or get acquired – the quicker, the better. Some of those companies are still around today, acquired by the likes of Canada Post, IBM, and Salesforce.

One of the things I cherish most from those days is the people I had the privilege of working alongside. This includes the manager who, to this day, I tout as the best manager I ever had. He was a mentor to me, and I hold him in very high regard. We're still good friends and have continued to work together over the years, bringing each other into projects as needed. It's a testament to the synergy and respect we have for each other.

I remember one Friday in particular because I had taken the day off to spend it with my 2-year-old, excited to pick up my new car. Shortly after I got home, the phone rang. It was my manager telling me I was laid off. Everybody had been told in person, but because I wasn't there, he had no option but to give me the bad news over the phone. He felt horrible because he knew I had just bought this new car. And I was instantly transported right back to that day when I was bawling my eyes out and walking to the bus, thinking to myself: "Here I am again."

The dot-com bubble had, indeed, burst.

But this time, something was different. Because this time, I knew what to do next.

When I worked at Compaq in the mid-to-late 90s, we were provided annual MAMOs that reflected the company's Mission, areas of Accountability, and how success would be Measured against your core Objectives.

We also had weekly APIT reports that tracked what was Accomplished, the next week's Priorities (driven by MAMOs), any outstanding or potential Issues, and any upcoming Travel or out-of-office plans.

Both these documents proved invaluable in highlighting what I did, how I did it, the results I drove, and how I overcame obstacles. In other words, I had all the information I needed at my fingertips to update my resume and tailor my cover letter.

Layoffs are a difficult but necessary part of the business world. They occur when companies have to reduce their workforce to remain profitable and competitive. Layoffs can be done for various reasons, such as financial hardship, restructuring, or changes in the industry. No matter the reason, layoffs result in employees losing their livelihood, causing significant disruption for those affected.

In my career, I've had head-hunters and recruitment companies ask me, "Why can't you hold down a job?" after seeing how much I've been bounced around.

I tell them that I'm such a great marketer that I've marketed myself out of every job I've had!

I've worked for scrappy startups and established enterprises: corporate conglomerates and mom-and-pop shops. Over the years, I realized that I thrive in start-ups, where there's lots going on, and you never know what you will be doing next. Change is constant.

And along with change – comes chaos.

But it's not for everyone. Some people thrive in a more structured role, where you are siloed in your lane, with little concern about what else is happening. You do your job. You do it well. You move up the corporate ladder. You're content. You get comfortable. You forget how to change.

What happens when you've outgrown your role, or worse, it becomes redundant? What happens when you get bored? Or get a new boss? Pay attention to the warning signs and prime yourself for change – whether it's within the company or somewhere new.

I once had a manager tell me that the sign of a good marketer is somebody who has not been in the same role for the same company for more than five years.

Maybe I practised this unknowingly.

So how do you recognize the writing on the wall?

Of all the warning signs, these are some of the most obvious clues to look out for:

- There will be more closed-door executive meetings than usual, often outside regular office hours.

- The HR, PR, Legal, IT, and Finance teams are either burning the midnight candle – or suddenly, MIA.

- Expenses will be more scrutinized.

- There will be more new faces walking around.

- You'll see HR walking around with yellow manilla envelopes.

As you spot the signs, begin to get your house in order. Clean up and organize your files. Gather and back up any CYA (cover your ass) emails and communications. If you use company assets, like laptops, cell phones, and tablets, remember that your company can do whatever it wants with the information stored.

Keep your personal world personal.

As crazy as this may sound, start preparing for your exit from day one by creating your MAMOs and APITs. Use them to keep your boss updated and, in the loop, – I promise they will appreciate the initiative.

- Update your accomplishments regularly on your resumé and also on LinkedIn.

- Build and surround yourself with a strong and powerful network – both business and personal.

- Stay in touch with your past managers with whom you share good relationships.

- Have regular performance reviews and ask your manager questions like: What am I doing right? Where do I need to improve? Where do I need to add value? What should I stop doing?

- Just as I advise companies – it's important to know who you help and how.

And finally...

The minute you start to have thoughts about being indispensable to the company – that's when the exit clock starts ticking. It then becomes a matter of what sparks the explosion – a decision made BY you – or one made FOR you.

Good managers are great.
Bad managers are better.

"A leader is one who knows the way, goes the way and shows the way."

- John Maxwell

While I have been blessed with some really great managers, I have also had my share of really awful ones. I recall one CEO in particular.

This CEO would regularly swagger (yes, swagger) into the office and declare: "I'm in the mood to fire someone today," after which he'd head to his office. It didn't take long before HR was in there too. And sure enough, by the end of the day, some poor soul was sacked.

And if you're wondering, yes, I eventually became that poor soul. Good riddance!

A good manager is someone who can lead with both authority and empathy. They know how to delegate tasks effectively and manage a team to maximize productivity and efficiency. Good managers understand the importance of communication and foster productive conversations between themselves and their employees or direct reports.

A good manager reflects a good team. There are no egos, the team thrives with each supporting the other, and everyone – particularly the company – reaps the benefits.

There's a saying I once heard that rings true in every job I've ever had, from Harvey's to JGC:

"Good managers lead by motivation. Bad managers lead by intimidation." - source unknown

Bad managers fail to lead their teams effectively and foster a negative work environment. They don't take the time to get to know their employees or provide clear direction and expectations. They fail to recognize and reward good performance, taking full credit for other people's efforts – and shifting full blame rather than taking responsibility for mistakes made or poor results.

As a result, employees become disengaged, morale drops, and productivity (as well as the bottom line) suffers.

Some people are great at seeing the big picture, strategizing, and managing complex, multi-faceted projects - but when it comes to people, they could be better.

Others are great at managing people but flail at managing projects. As a result, it's not uncommon for companies to struggle with how to best motivate and retain great talent when it's recognized. Rather than risk losing these shining stars, they get promoted to being a manager – without being taught how to manage people effectively.

* *

A good manager reflects a good team. There are no egos, the team thrives with each supporting the other, and everyone – particularly the company – reaps the benefits.

* *

When you promote an excellent salesperson to a manager role, for example, you may lose a great salesperson and gain a bad manager. They're still very good at their job, but suddenly with people to manage, they don't know what to do. So they do what they have always done without the support and training to properly help, coach, and guide their team. Done poorly, the transition from colleague to manager can lead to resentment, back-stabbing, and a toxic workplace.

That's when things start to fall apart.

* *

When you promote an excellent salesperson to a manager role, for example, you may lose a great salesperson and gain a bad manager. They're still very good at their job, but suddenly they now have people to manage, and don't know what to do.

* *

I remember having a manager who was amazing at managing projects but not so great at managing people. While we clashed as boss and subordinate (her words, not mine), I became friends with her after I had left the company. In hindsight, I recognize the obstacles she must have been facing as a female in a senior role at a technology company in the 90s.

Key characteristics of a good leader

There are many traits that define a good leader. Here are five important qualities that I believe are essential for effective leadership:

1. Visionary: A good leader has a clear vision of where they want their organization to go and how they plan to get there. They can articulate their vision to others and inspire them to work towards achieving it. According to a study by Deloitte, 94% of executives believe that having a clear vision and purpose is essential for effective leadership.

2. Communication: Communication is critical to effective leadership. A good leader can communicate their vision, goals, and expectations clearly and concisely to their team. They can also listen to feedback from their team and incorporate it into their decision-making process. A survey by Interact/Harris Poll found that 91% of employees believe that effective communication is the top attribute of successful leaders.

3. Integrity: A good leader leads by example and sets a high standard for ethical behavior. They are honest, transparent, and trustworthy in all their dealings with others. According to the Edelman Trust Barometer, 76% of employees believe that ethical leadership is the most important factor in building trust within an organization.

4. Empathy: A good leader is able to put themselves in their team members' shoes and understand their

perspectives. They are supportive and caring towards their team members and strive to create a positive work environment. Research conducted by Development Dimensions International (DDI) indicates that leaders who display empathy are more likely to have engaged employees, resulting in a 40% increase in discretionary effort.

5. Adaptability: A good leader can adapt to changing circumstances and make decisions quickly when needed. They are able to navigate uncertainty and complexity with ease and maintain focus on their goals. A global leadership study by Korn Ferry found that 90% of high-performing leaders demonstrate strong adaptability.

5 Ways Good Leaders Motivate and Instill Confidence

Good leaders motivate their teams by creating a positive work environment that fosters creativity, innovation, and growth. They provide their team members with the tools and resources they need to be successful and recognize their achievements and contributions.

They instil confidence in their team members by leading by example and being accountable for their actions. They are transparent and honest in their communication and create a culture of trust and respect within their organization. Here are five ways....

1. Recognition: Good leaders recognize their team members' achievements and contributions and celebrate their successes.

2. Support: Good leaders provide their team members with the support they need to succeed, whether through training, mentorship, or other resources.

3. Feedback: Good leaders provide constructive feedback to their team members to help them improve and grow.

4. Trust: Good leaders create a culture of trust and respect within their organization by being transparent and honest in their communication.

5. Empowerment: Good leaders empower their team members to take ownership of their work and make decisions that support the organization's goals.

To become a great leader, seek opportunities to develop and hone these essential qualities. Through refinement, continuous learning, self-reflection, and practice, individuals can become successful leaders who inspire and empower their teams to flourish.

Identifying Red Flags: Traits and Behaviors of Ineffective Leaders

Unfortunately, not all leaders are effective. There are certain traits and behaviours that make for a poor leader. Here are five red flags to look for:

1. Ego: A bad leader is often driven by their ego and is more concerned with their own success than that of their organization or team.

2. Lack of Communication: A bad leader is often poor at communicating their vision and goals to their team members. They may also be dismissive of feedback and input from others.

3. Micromanagement: A bad leader may be overly controlling and micromanage their team members, stifling creativity and innovation.

4. Lack of Accountability: A bad leader may be unwilling to take responsibility for their actions or decisions and blame others for their mistakes.

5. Poor Ethics: A bad leader may engage in unethical behavior, such as lying, cheating, or stealing.

A study by Gallup found that organizations with high employee engagement outperform those with low employee engagement by 21% in profitability and 17% in productivity." - Gallup, "State of the Global Workplace," 2021.

Addressing Leadership Misalignment: Strategies for Navigating the Wrong Fit

When you find yourself in a situation where you have the wrong person in a leadership role, it can be a challenging and delicate issue to address. Taking proactive steps to rectify the situation is essential for the health of your company, your other employees, and your peace of mind. Here are some strategies to help navigate this challenging scenario:

1. Evaluate and Assess the Situation: As you assess the individual's performance and their fit for the leadership role, identify specific areas where they may be falling short or lacking any necessary skills and qualities. This evaluation should be based on objective criteria and feedback from stakeholders, team members, and other leaders within the organization.

2. Provide Constructive Feedback: It's crucial to provide the individual with honest and constructive feedback. Schedule a meeting to discuss your concerns, focusing on specific instances or behaviors that have raised red flags. Offer guidance and support in areas where improvement is needed and provide resources or development opportunities to help them grow in their role.

3. Offer Additional Training and Support: In some cases, the person may lack the necessary skills or experience for the leadership position. Providing resources and support can be a valuable investment in their professional development, as well as the organization's success. Consider mentoring, coaching, training and/or courses to help them learn the required competencies.

4. Seek a Role Redefinition or Reallocation: If it becomes apparent that the individual is consistently unable to fulfill the expectations of the leadership role, it may be necessary to redefine or reallocate their responsibilities. This approach allows them to contribute in a capacity that aligns better with their strengths and interests while also allowing the organization to bring in a more suitable leader for the original role.

5. Transition with Sensitivity: In cases where a change in leadership is unavoidable, it is crucial to manage the transition with sensitivity and professionalism. Offer support to the individual during this period, whether it's providing assistance with their new role or helping them with their exit from the organization if necessary. Communicate openly and transparently with the team about the change, highlighting the company's commitment to finding the right leader to drive success.

6. Focus on Leadership Succession Planning: Prevent future situations of having the wrong person in a leadership role by prioritizing leadership succession planning. Identify and build a database of high-potential individuals within your organization and provide them with opportunities to develop their skills, thus creating a pipeline of qualified candidates for leadership positions. This proactive approach helps ensure the organization has the right leaders in place when needed.

7. Learn from the Experience: Every situation, however good or bad, is an opportunity to learn and grow. Reflect on the factors that contributed to having the wrong person in a leadership role and use those insights to refine your selection and evaluation processes. Consider incorporating assessments, interviews, and reference

checks to gain a comprehensive understanding of a candidate's qualifications and fit for the role.

While dealing with the wrong person in a leadership role can be challenging, addressing the situation promptly and effectively is crucial for the organization's success. By employing these strategies, you can navigate the situation with professionalism, respect, and a commitment to finding the best leadership fit for the organization's needs.

Embracing the Power of Good Leadership

The impact of good leadership vs. bad is significant, affecting employee morale, productivity, and overall organizational success. Good leaders possess qualities such as vision, communication, integrity, empathy, and adaptability. They motivate and instil confidence in their teams by creating a positive work environment, providing support and feedback, building trust, and empowering their team members. On the other hand, bad leaders often display traits such as ego, poor communication, micromanagement, lack of accountability, and poor ethics.

With both ends of the spectrum as a frame of reference, you can distinguish between the warning signs and the welcome signs as you meet your next leader – or become one yourself.

Reflections and Musings

"The journey into self-love and self-acceptance must begin with self-examination until you take the journey of self-reflection, it is impossible to grow or learn in life."

- Iyanla Vanzant

Times have drastically changed. We grew up in an era of fewer choices, but today we are spoiled with options – food, entertainment, technology, travel, and even career.

If I wasn't a marketer, one thing is for sure: I'd be doing something that embodies creativity and logic.

Growing up, I was fascinated with make-up's ability to change anyone into just about anything. For as long as I can remember, I longed to be a special effects makeup artist!!

I used to love doing makeup on Halloween. I loved seeing the transformation and the opportunity it gave me to unleash my creativity. While never great at life drawing, I thrived playing with textures, patterns, formulas, layouts, and grids.

This seeped into my professional career, first as a graphic designer, then as a corporate marketer, and finally as an agency owner.

I was a conflicted girl when it came time to pick an academic path after graduating high school. I was as excited by Computer Science as I was by Art. So, when it was time to decide, I applied for both. I figured whichever accepted me first was the track I was meant to follow. As luck –perhaps fate – would have it, I was welcomed into the Graphic Design program, where I flourished at balancing both the technical and creative courses in an intense, 3-year program. By now, we all know what happened next.

* *

How can I do as much as possible in the shortest time – and how can I benefit the most from that time? It's a trait I apply constantly throughout my personal and professional life.

You will never find me sitting idle. That's my nature. Even when I'm relaxing or watching TV, in between commercial breaks, I pick up my phone and play a game to see if I can reach the next level in those few minutes. Or I listen to a podcast while exercising or music while cooking – with bonus points for dancing!

Even walking into my kitchen to prepare breakfast, my mind is constantly optimizing the workflow – calculating what tasks to do first based on which takes the longest. Call it being proactive. Call it competitive. Call it OCD. Efficiency drives me.

While studies have shown that nothing gets done correctly if you do too many things simultaneously, I've found that when you combine tasks that complement each other, you can multitask and be efficient – but just like everything in life, you have to know your limits.

* *

"Believe in your heart that you're meant to live a life full of passion, purpose, magic and miracles." – Roy T. Bennett

* *

Faithfulness is a character trait I value highly. It is thinly separated by loyalty and staying true to your word, values, and morals. I can be pretty stubborn in this aspect – hanging onto my convictions. I am passionate about having a consistent and cohesive story that everyone, from the floor sweeper to the CEO, can easily articulate as the foundation of B2B marketing success. At times, it's gotten me in trouble, but it speaks volumes about my approach to brands and messaging.

In our brainstorming sessions, creative briefings, and client meetings, we contribute randomly and in a non-linear manner, emptying our thoughts. That's where we start seeing and connecting the dots. The ability to voice my judgement and opinion with utmost confidence comes from the fact that I've assessed the situation in totality. My clients value this collaboration – it puts us all on the same page towards a common goal.

Showing empathy and compassion is what I also practice, particularly in hostile and potentially volatile situations.

Which brings us to the topic of ruthless honesty.

I embrace criticism as long as it is constructive. The trick is knowing how to be constructive while simultaneously being honest and kind. Yes, it's important to "call a spade a spade" and not beat around the bush, but it's easy to trigger negative, defensive reactions. This often happens when communicating client feedback to designers who have poured their heart into their creativity, whether it's a social media image, a logo, or an entire website.

But clients don't always like the work, which often comes down to subjective opinion – despite an approved brief, concept, and/ or strategy. Framing and delivering the feedback positively and pinpointing what worked, as well as the rationale behind any changes, guides the team on where to adapt, refine, and in some cases, start over.

How feedback is delivered, as well as received, can fuel a team to work together towards a common goal – or foster hostility and negativity that fractures success.

* *

After returning from a vacation in Jamaica, I imagined myself stranded on an island resort. My first thought was: "How long would I be here?"

A week? A month? A year? Longer?

What would I miss the most? Would I have my gadgets around to listen to music or watch TV?

Would I have the internet?

If you've ever taken an extended leave from work, you get it. For me, the first time I was "stranded on a desert island" was during maternity leave. Overnight, you are cut off from your daily routine of work, your office, and your colleagues, and you get into a different zone.

You can't prepare for how you're impacted. Some easily disconnect from work, while others need to check in regularly. How long it takes for that transition varies from person to person. I'm fortunate that I had nine months off for each of my three maternity leaves. While I must admit it was torture at first, by the time I had my third, I had the exit, acclamation, and re-entry process nailed.

I feel that the ability to accept and adapt to any given situation is what matters most when faced with life's forks in the road – planned or otherwise.

Gratitude and Growth - My Journey with You

As I sit here, penning the final chapter of *Thriving in Chaos - Lessons Learned as a Corporate Marketer*, my heart is overflowing with gratitude for the incredible people who have shaped my journey. It is impossible to fully capture in words the immense impact each of you has had on my career and personal growth. But I will try my best to express my heartfelt appreciation.

First and foremost, I want to thank my husband, Dan. Your unwavering support, love, and understanding have been the bedrock of my success. Through the late nights and countless weekends spent working, you stood by me, always encouraging me to pursue my passions. Your belief in me gave me the strength to persevere through the chaos and emerge stronger than ever.

To our children, Brayden, Ethan, Jordan, Sean, and Zach, thank you for your love, support, and inspiration. You have taught me the true meaning of balance and reminded me of the importance of cherishing the moments that matter most.

To my family and friends, your unwavering support has been an incredible source of strength. Thank you for being my cheerleaders, lending a listening ear, and providing invaluable advice. Your belief in me, even when I doubted myself, has been a constant reminder of the power of a strong support network.

To my colleagues and mentors, I am forever grateful for the opportunities you have provided me and the wisdom you have shared. Each of you has played a pivotal role in shaping my marketing career. Your guidance, encouragement, and willingness to challenge me pushed me to step outside my comfort zone and unlock my true potential.

To my good bosses, thank you for recognizing my skills and fostering an environment of growth. Your trust and belief in my abilities gave me the confidence to take risks, explore new avenues, and flourish in my professional journey.

And to my bad bosses, while our time together may have been challenging, I choose to view those experiences as opportunities for growth. Through adversity, I developed resilience and learned valuable lessons that have shaped me into the leader I am today. I am grateful for the tough times, as they taught me the importance of perseverance and standing up for what I believe in.

Finally, to the industry I am so passionate about, thank you for providing a canvas for me to express my creativity, intellect, and love for print. Your ever-evolving landscape has kept me on my toes, embracing change and finding innovative ways to navigate the chaos.

As I close this chapter, I want each and every one of you to know that your impact on my life is immeasurable. Without your love, support, and guidance, I would not have been able to write this book, sharing my journey and the lessons I have learned along the way. Together, we have shown that amidst the chaos, one can find the strength to thrive.

With heartfelt gratitude,

Joanne – B2B marketer who's passionate about print.

References

Preface:

Stephen Covey

https://veeroesquotes.com/what-you-do-has/

https://en.wikipedia.org/wiki/Stephen_Covey

https://www.franklincovey.com/the-7-habits/

W.D Edwards

https://industryforum.co.uk/blog/in-god-we-trust-all-others-must-bring-data/

https://www.bl.uk/people/w-edwards-deming

Marshall Goldsmith's book "What Got You Here, Won't Get You There"

https://marshallgoldsmith.com/book-page-what-got-you-here/

https://amzn.eu/d/j91FnQN

About the Author:

Montreal, Canada

https://en.wikipedia.org/wiki/Culture_of_Montreal

https://designyoutrust.com/2019/05/cool-old-photos-show-what-school-looked-like-in-the-1970s/

What can go wrong, will go wrong:

Pareto's principle:

https://en.wikipedia.org/wiki/Pareto_principle

Opinions are like assholes – everybody has one:

Dr. W. Edwards Deming:

https://en.wikipedia.org/wiki/W._Edwards_Deming

https://deming.org/explore/fourteen-points/

Post-It Story:

https://www.ideatovalue.com/insp/nickskillicorn/2017/04/true-story-post-notes-almost-failed/

The Viagra Story:

https://www.drugs.com/slideshow/viagra-little-blue-pill-1043#:~:text=The%20sildenafil%20compound%20was%20originally,inducing%20erections%20than%20treating%20angina.

Setting up multiple goal posts:

Steve Jobs quote:

https://www.creativethinkinghub.com/steve-jobs-was-right-real-artists-ship/#:~:text=Steve%20Jobs%20famously%20said%3B%20%E2%80%9CReal,you%20do%20something%20with%20it.

How to stretch your time – and money:

Express Employment Professionals Survey:

https://www.expresspros.com/

University of Minnesota Research Study:

http://www.psychologicalscience.org/news/releases/tidy-desk-or-messy-desk-each-has-its-

benefits.html#.WWJ_j9PyuWY

McKinsey & Company Report:

https://www.mckinsey.com/industries/high-

tech/our-insights/the-social-economy

The significance of 121:

The Power of Subconscious Mind by Dr. Joseph Murphy

https://amzn.eu/d/38W1Z5Y

You're fired! Now what?

New York Times Report:

https://www.nytimes.com/2023/02/07/business/zoom-layoffs.html

Entrepreneur.com Report:

https://www.entrepreneur.com/en-in/news-and-trends/disney-plans-to-fire-7000-employees-report/444650

Peek under the hood:

Good to Great by Jim Collins

https://amzn.eu/d/elHxVp2

https://www.jimcollins.com/